CW01065284

Devotions to Our Lady
of Perpetual Succour

Originally compiled by W. Raemers CSsR
Revised by Glynn MacNiven-Johnston

*All booklets are published thanks to the
generous support of the members of the
Catholic Truth Society*

CATHOLIC TRUTH SOCIETY
PUBLISHERS TO THE HOLY SEE

Contents

All rights reserved. First published 2014 by The Incorporated Catholic Truth Society, 40-46 Harleyford Road London SE11 5AY Tel: 020 7640 0042 Fax: 020 7640 0046. © 2014 The Incorporated Catholic Truth Society.

ISBN 978 1 86082 928 4

~ PREFACE ~

When Pope Francis created me a cardinal, to my delight he assigned the Church of the Most Holy Redeemer and St Alphonsus in Via Merulana as my Titular Church in Rome. This lovely church, as you may know, houses the original image of Our Lady of Perpetual Succour, which, now widely reproduced, is venerated in churches throughout the world. It movingly depicts the Christ-child, his redeeming Passion already in view, tenderly clasping his blessed Mother's hand. Mary looks upon her son with such loving compassion. The image has inspired, and still inspires, immense comfort and hope in the hearts of millions. Devotion to Our Lady of Perpetual Succour powerfully helps the Church's universal mission to lead everyone into that joy flowing from a living relationship with Jesus. I therefore very much welcome this new edition of devotions to Our Lady of Perpetual Succour published by the CTS. When you use it, please pray for me too, that helped by the motherly intercession and love of Our Lady, I may faithfully serve her Son, our Most Holy Redeemer. Thank you.

✝ Cardinal Vincent Nichols
(Archbishop of Westminster)

Our Lady of
~Perpetual Succour~

Jesus said to his mother, 'Woman, this is your son.' Then to his disciple he said, 'This is your mother.'

(Jn 19:26-27)

With these words from the cross, Christ gave his mother to be the mother not only of the apostle John but of all Christians - of the whole Church. She is there to help us, just as she was at Cana, when she interceded with her son for the family who hadn't provided enough wine for their wedding guests.

The Blessed Virgin Mary has demonstrated her tender care for us throughout history. She has appeared in paintings, statues and in person to remind us of God's love for us and of her willingness to intercede for us.

She does not appear on her own account, but to help us to learn to be disciples as she herself was the perfect disciple. Each time she appears she emphasises something that will help us.

The Icon

This icon was painted in the fourteenth or fifteenth century; it was given the name *Mater de Perpetuo Succursu* in 1867 by Pope Pius IX. The name is literally translated into English as Mother of Perpetual Help, but it is also variously rendered as Our Lady of Perpetual Succour and Our Lady of Perpetual Help. This name reminds us that when we need help, the Virgin Mary will be there to guide us to see God's presence in our problems or suffering. The icon reminds us she saw her own son die in a cruel and horrible manner. She understands suffering and she is with us to support us in the suffering of our lives.

An icon is more than just a Christian religious painting. In the Orthodox tradition, icons are venerated. An icon is not art: an icon is somewhere God is present. Icon painters therefore painted with this in mind, praying and fasting. Because they represent the Divine, icons carry something Divine in them and because of this and their close links with the Orthodox liturgy, the types and styles of icons are more set than are the subjects of western art. This specific type of icon traces its roots to an original, now lost, traditionally believed to have been painted by St Luke. This representation is known as the *Hodegetria* in Greek, meaning *She who shows the Way.* Our Lady holds the child Jesus in her left hand, and gestures towards her son with her right, indicating to us that the Way is through Jesus Christ, Son of God, son of Mary.

This particular icon is recognisably from Crete, which at the time had a famous school of icon painters. Western influences are evident in the icon. Traditionally, icons show Our Lady *Theotokos* (God-bearer, Mother of God) wearing imperial purple, but here her robes are dark blue. Following the western tradition, the painter has used ultramarine (crushed lapis lazuli), the most expensive pigment of the time; yellow varnish and age have darkened it. The Eastern Church created few icons emphasising the Passion, but Crete was at that time part of the Venetian Republic, and Cretan icon painters had both western influences and western customers.

The icon of Our Lady of Perpetual Succour also differs from a typical *Hodegetria* icon in the pose of the child Jesus. Here we see the child Jesus, dressed in gold (emphasising that he is Son of God and the Light), placing his hands into those of his mother, but he is turned to face the Archangel Gabriel in the top right corner who displays the cross to him. Gabriel has his hands covered to indicate the holiness of the object that he carries (as still happens today in solemn liturgy in both Orthodox and Catholic rites). Meanwhile, the Archangel Michael carries the instruments of the Passion - the lance that pierced Jesus's side, the sponge on the hyssop stick, the pot of vinegar and gall, and the nails for the crucifixion.

The child's sandal is falling off. This may be a reference to the book of Ruth (*Rt* 4:8) where a sandal represented ownership. The sandal falls to earth, reclaiming creation for Christ. Another interpretation sees the falling sandal as Christ giving up his dignity as God to enter into our humanity (See Philippians 2:6-11).

As is usual in Orthodox icons, the saints each have the abbreviated versions of their names inscribed in Greek letters in red enabling us to read the titles of Mary, Mother of God MP ΘY; Jesus Christ IC XC; Archangel Michael Ὁ AP M; and Archangel Gabriel Ὁ AP Γ.

Our Lady looks steadily at us, drawing us into a dialogue with her, inviting us to follow the gesture of her hands as she offers us her son Jesus. We see his whole body turned to that of his mother, his hands in hers; but his face is set to the cross.

Our Lady fills most of the painted space denoting her immense importance and ability to help us. She is our Mother. This is the perpetual succour we can rely on - the help of a mother who loves us. We can rely on her in all our sufferings, knowing that she has also experienced great suffering and that she did not run away from the cross.

Sometimes darkness has its hour, but we are called not to run away from it but to resist the hatred or despair or anger that comes with it, just as Mary stood at the foot of the cross, not despairing but sharing Christ's suffering, and by her faith battling the forces of evil.

This small icon (it measures only 43cms by 53cms) powerfully reminds us of our Mother's concern for us and her consolation and help in times of difficulties.

The History of the Icon

It is said this icon was brought to Rome by a merchant and that after his death it was given to St Matthew's church on the Via Merulana. St Matthew's was a simple church dating from the fifth century and served by Irish Augustinians. Records show the icon was first publicly venerated there in 1499. At that time called the Madonna of St Matthew, the icon soon became very popular, with large numbers of pilgrims every year making their way to pray there. Many miracles and cures were reported. The icon was a focus of prayer in St Matthew's until the late eighteenth century; in 1798, however, the short-lived Roman Republic was proclaimed by Napoleon's troops who had invaded the city and forced Pope Pius VI into exile in France.

During this time many churches were destroyed, including St Matthew's. But the icon was saved, and for many years hung in a side chapel of the (since demolished) church of St Mary's in the Postern Gate (Santa Maria in Posterula) where the Irish Augustinians had moved when St Matthew's was destroyed. The icon was hung in a side chapel because the main altar already had a representation of Our Lady of Grace. Gradually, the Madonna of St Matthew was almost forgotten.

The Icon and the Redemptorists

In 1853 Pope Pius IX invited the Redemptorists to open a house in Rome. The Redemptorists (the Congregation of the Most Holy Redeemer) were founded in 1732 by Alphonsus Liguori to preach the Word of God to the poor. They preach often on prayer and on the intercession of Our Lady who their constitution calls a "perpetual help". St Alphonsus said of her, "Joyfully honour and love this good lady. Continue faithfully in your devotion to her and you will never be lost."

By the mid 1800s, the order had grown so much it was decided its general headquarters should move to Rome. The order bought the Villa Caetani and its land to build a Generalate House, and a church to be consecrated to the Most Holy Redeemer and also named for St Alphonsus Liguori. In 1862, a historian from the Curia told a group of Redemptorists that he had discovered the land they had built the church on was the site of an older church, St Matthew's, where there had been a miraculous icon but that unfortunately it was now lost.

One of the men listening was Michele Marchi. He had been an altar boy at Santa Maria in Posterula and knew that the icon was there. The Redemptorists felt inspired to ask for the return of the icon to the site where it had been venerated for three centuries.

The Redemptorists' Superior General of the time, Fr Nicolas Mauron, was a friend of the Pope's and asked him to intercede for them with the Augustinians who held the icon. Pope Pius IX was convinced the icon should be exposed to public veneration again, in the church now standing on the same site as its original home. He directed the Augustinians to give the icon to the Redemptorists and told the Redemptorists to replace the icon in the Augustinian church with another picture to be hung in its place.

The Redemptorists had never seen the icon but, when they went to collect it, were amazed to find it had echoes of their Congregation's coat of arms which shows the lance, hyssop stick and sponge on either side of the cross with the initials of Jesus and Mary.

The icon had been neglected and its colours were faded, so a Polish artist was brought in to restore it. In 1866, the icon of Our Lady of Perpetual Succour was taken in procession to the Church of St Alphonsus, and several miraculous cures were reported as it passed through the streets. The most famous of these were a small boy cured of meningitis and a young girl who regained the use of her paralysed leg.

In May of the same year, Pope Pius IX came to visit the icon and solemnly entrusted the Redemptorists with the task of making it known to the whole world.

In June 1867 the icon was "crowned". Gold crowns were placed over the heads of Christ and his mother. The Virgin's crown had twenty-six precious stones, and more gold and stones were added later.

The icon of Our Lady of Perpetual Succour still hangs in the Church of St Alphonsus (Sant' Alfonso Liguori). Interestingly, this church has several British connections. The architect of this church, George Wigley, was British (and a founder member of the Society of St Vincent de Paul) and the entire building was paid for from the private fortune of a British Redemptorist, Fr Edward Douglas, a member of the family of the Marquess of Queensbury. Also, as of February 2014, it is the titular church of Vincent Nichols, Cardinal Archbishop of Westminster.

In the 1990s the church was reordered and the icon was found to be in bad condition. It was taken down for restoration. The gold crowns and jewels were removed to stop further damage to the paint and to return the icon to something more like its original state. At the same time it underwent various tests which showed the wood it was painted on could be dated to somewhere between 1325 and 1480. The actual painting was more difficult to date, as over the years there had been a lot of over-painting and repairs; but given the icon was on public display from 1499, a similar time-frame may be presumed.

Make her known throughout the world

The Redemptorists took the Pope's exhortation seriously and when they were asked to establish a mission church in Roxbury near Boston in the United States, they took with them a copy of the icon which had been touched to the original. Since then, over two thousand further copies have been painted, touched to the original and taken to Redemptorist houses throughout the world. In Roxbury so many cures were reported that, in March 1901, the *New York Times* called it "the Lourdes of America".

Redemptorist missionaries took another copy of the icon to the Philippines in 1906 and the devotion grew there so that in 1958 a national shrine was opened in Baclaran. Other places where the icon is especially venerated include Ireland, Poland, Mexico, Brazil and Haiti where Our Lady of Perpetual Succour is the country's patron.

In the 1920s, in St Louis Missouri, a novena to Our Lady of Perpetual Succour was started. This devotion was taken up in other churches and has since spread worldwide.

The Feast of Our Lady of Perpetual Succour is kept in Redemptorist churches on the Sunday preceding 24th June, the Feast of St John the Baptist; and in other places on 27th June.

* With thanks to Rachel Sim for information about icon painting.

~ Devotions ~

Morning Prayer

Most holy and Immaculate Virgin and our Mother Mary, you are our Perpetual Help, our refuge and our hope. We come to you today. We thank God for all the graces received through your intercession. Mother of Perpetual Help, we promise to love you always and to do all we can to lead others to you. Confident of your powerful influence with God, obtain for us these graces: the strength to overcome temptation, a perfect love for Jesus Christ, and a holy death so that we will live with you and your Son for all eternity. Amen.

Invocations

O Mother of Perpetual Succour, you whose very name inspires confidence,

Response: help me, loving Mother.

That I may be victorious in the trying time of temptation, **R.**

That I may rise again, should I fall into sin, **R.**

That I may break any bonds of Satan in which I become entangled, **R.**

Against corrupting companions and media, **R.**

That I return to my former fervour,
if I become lukewarm, **R.**

In my preparation for the sacraments
and the performance of my Christian duties, **R.**

In all the trials and troubles of life, **R.**

Against my own inconstancy, that I may persevere to the end, **R.**

That I may inspire others to love and serve you, **R.**

To my last hour, to my last breath, **R.**

Act of Consecration to Our Lady of Perpetual Succour

O Mother of Perpetual Succour, and my own best beloved Mother, I thank you for all the blessings and graces you have obtained for me since my birth, and especially during all my temptations. And now, to so many former favours, vouchsafe, O Mary, add that of admitting me, though most unworthy, into the number of your special clients, that with them I may prove to you my devotion of veneration and love. You shall always be, next after God, my only hope, and the object most dear to my heart. In all my wants, in all my straits and temptations, I will always have recourse to you; you shall be my refuge and my consolation. I desire in all the combats, afflictions and weariness of life to have no other support but God and you. I would rather be one of your servants than have the whole world at my command; my ambition shall be to serve you, to bless you, to love you till my dying breath. Amen.

Litany of Our Lady of Perpetual Succour

Lord have mercy on us.
Lord have mercy on us.
Christ have mercy on us.
Christ have mercy on us.
Christ hear us.
Christ graciously hear us.
God, the Father of heaven,
have mercy on us.
Holy Trinity, one God,
have mercy on us.
Holy Mary,
pray for us.
Holy Virgin, conceived without sin,
pray for us.
Our Lady of Perpetual Succour,
pray for us.
We sinners call to you,
Mary, help us.

That we may love God with our whole hearts, **R.**

That we may be conformable in all things
to your Divine Son, **R.**

That we may have a tender and heart-felt devotion to
you, most holy Virgin, **R.**

That we may hate sin, **R.**

That we may frequently remember our last end, **R.**

That we may often and worthily receive
the sacraments, **R.**

That we may avoid occasions of sin, **R.**

That we may not neglect prayer, **R.**

That we turn to prayer in the hour of temptation, **R.**

That we may forgive our enemies, **R.**

That we may not defer our conversion, **R.**

That we may strive to overcome our bad habits, **R.**

That we may live and die in the grace of God, **R.**

In all concerns of soul and body, **R.**

In sickness and pain, **R.**

In struggles against the inclination of corrupt nature, **R.**

In assaults of evil spirits, **R.**

In temptations against purity, **R.**

In all danger of sinning, **R.**

When we have reached the end of our earthly course, **R.**

When we breathe forth our spirits into the hands of our Creator, **R.**

When our souls appear before our Divine Judge, **R.**

Lamb of God, you take away the sins of the world, *spare us, O Lord.*
Lamb of God, you take away the sins of the world, *graciously hear us, O Lord.*
Lamb of God, you take away the sins of the world, *have mercy on us.*

V.   Pray for us O Holy Mother of God.

R.   That we may be made worthy of the promises of Christ.

O God, who have willed that the mother of your only-begotten Son should be the perpetual succour of Christians on earth, grant us grace to call on her with confidence in all our necessities of soul and body, so that saved through her protection and assistance, we may be brought to the everlasting vision of your glory in heaven. Through Jesus Christ our Lord. Amen.

Prayer for Perseverance

O Mother of Perpetual Succour, grant that I remain faithful to you till my dying breath. Amen.

— The Perpetual Novena —

Prayers to Our Lady of Perpetual Succour

First Prayer

OMother of Perpetual Succour, behold me, a miserable sinner, at your feet. I have recourse to you, and put my trust in you. O Mother of Mercy, have pity upon me. I hear you called by all the refuge and hope of sinners; be then my refuge and my hope. Succour me for the love of Jesus Christ; stretch out your hand to me, O my Mother, who recommend and dedicate myself to you as your perpetual servant. I bless and thank God for having in his mercy given to me this confidence in you, the pledge, as I believe, of my eternal salvation. Alas, too often in the past I have miserably fallen because I did have not recourse to you! I know that with your help I shall conquer; I know that you will help me if I recommend myself to you; but I fear that in the occasions of falling I might not call on you and so should lose my soul. This, then, is the grace I seek from you - and I beg you to obtain it for me - namely, in the assaults of hell always to have recourse to you and to say to you: O Mary, help me; Mother of Perpetual Succour, do not allow me to be separated from God.

Nine Hail Marys

Ant. Holy Mary, succour the miserable, help the faint-hearted, cheer those that weep, pray for the people, be the advocate of the clergy, intercede for all women consecrated to God. Let all who implore your perpetual succour feel your aid.

V. O Lady, you have been made a refuge for us.

Let us pray. O almighty and merciful God, who have given us the picture of your most Blessed Mother to venerate under the title of Perpetual Succour, grant that, amid all the changes of our journey through life, we may be so defended by the continual protection of the same immaculate ever-virgin Mary that we may deserve to obtain the rewards of your eternal redemption. Who lives and reigns with God the Father in the unity of the Holy Spirit, world without end. Amen.

Second prayer

O Mother of Perpetual Succour, grant that I may always invoke your most powerful name, for your name is help in life, salvation in death. Mary most pure, Mary most sweet, let your name henceforth be the breath of my life. O Lady, do not be slow to come to my succour whenever I call on you; for in all the wants which befall me, I will never cease to call on you, and to repeat again and again: Mary, Mary! What comfort, what sweetness, what confidence, what tenderness my soul feels at the mere mention of your name, at the very thought of you! I thank the Lord for having given me for my good this name, so sweet, so amiable, so powerful. But merely to pronounce your name is not enough for me. I wish to do so out of love. I wish that love may remind me always to call you Mother of Perpetual Succour.

Nine Hail Marys etc.

Third prayer

O Mother of Perpetual Succour, you are the dispenser of all the graces which God bestows on us wretched creatures; and for this he made you so powerful, so rich, so kind, so that you may succour us in our miseries. You are the advocate of the most miserable and abandoned sinners, who have recourse to you; help me, then, who recommend myself to you. I place my eternal salvation in your hands, to you I consign my soul. Number me among your more special servants; take me under your protection, and I will be satisfied. Yes, for if you help me, I fear nothing, not even my sins; since you will obtain for me the pardon of them; nor the devils, for you are more powerful than all hell; nor even Jesus, my true judge, because by one prayer of yours he will be appeased. My only fear is that through my own negligence I should cease to recommend myself to you, and so should be lost. Obtain for me, my Lady, the pardon of my sins, the love of Jesus, final perseverance, and the grace of always having recourse to you, O Mother of Perpetual Succour.

Nine Hail Marys etc.

Perpetual Novena Prayers with a Leader

Opening Hymn: *Immaculate Mary*

Leader: Let us kneel as we gather together to honour our Mother and our Perpetual Help. We recall how she helped others. Her whole life was a lesson in love.

All: Mother of Perpetual Help, today we face so many difficulties. Your picture tells us so much about you. It reminds us to reach out and help those in need. Help us understand that our lives belong to others as much as they belong to us. Mary, model of Christian love, we know we cannot heal every ill or solve every problem, but with God's grace, we intend to do what we can. May we be true witnesses to the world that love for one another really matters. May our daily actions proclaim how fully our lives are modelled after yours, Mother of Perpetual Help.

Leader: Mary, you were a woman of steadfast faith. Your faith in Jesus never wavered. Model of all believers, pray to the Holy Spirit for us. Help us not only to accept all your Son teaches us, but to put that teaching into practice.

All: Mother of Perpetual Help, as a child, Jesus ran to you for comfort and reassurance. You did not see him as only a frail child. Moved by the Holy Spirit, you accepted Jesus as the Son of the Most High, the long-awaited Messiah. Following your example of faith, help us recognise Jesus in those we meet, especially the poor and the lonely, the sick and the elderly. Keep us always mindful, dear Mother, that whatever we do to the least of our brothers and sisters, we do to your loving Son. May his words live in our hearts and influence our lives and the lives of those we meet.

Leader: Let us pray to be open to God's Word.

All: Mary, woman of faith, you pondered and treasured the meaning of God's words and actions in your life. You generously responded to his Word in faith. As we listen to God's Word, help us be attentive to his message. May the Holy Spirit enlighten our understanding and give us the courage to put these words into practice.

Leader: Let us stand as we present our petitions: grant wisdom and guidance to our Holy Father, Pope N., our Bishop N., our priests, and all the leaders of our nation, state, and community.

All: May your mother intercede for us, Lord.

Leader: Grant peace and unity throughout the world, especially in our homes and families.

All: May your mother intercede for us, Lord.

Leader: Grant that young people respond generously to the call of the Holy Spirit in deepening their faith and choosing their vocation in life.

All: May your mother intercede for us, Lord.

Leader: Grant us continued health of mind and body, and help the sick, especially . . . to regain their health according to your holy will.

All: May your mother intercede for us, Lord.

Leader: Grant eternal rest to all our deceased, especially . . . and to the souls of all the faithful departed.

All: May your mother intercede for us, Lord.

Leader: Let us pause now silently to present our own personal petitions to Our Mother of Perpetual Help.

Leader: Let us kneel as we continue our prayers:

All: Mary, humble handmaid of the Lord, we need your example today to discover God's will in our lives. You always gave God the first place in your life. Just as you pondered his Word in your heart, help each of us to seek his plan in all that we do. Give us the conviction that nothing is more important than doing the will of our heavenly Father. May we spend each moment in loving and pleasing him. Help us follow your example in proclaiming, I am the servant of the Lord, I will what God wills, when he wills it, as he wills it, because he wills it.

Leader: Mother of Perpetual Help, your picture reminds us that we are to carry our cross as Jesus did. With courage, he endured injustice, abandonment and betrayal, pain and suffering, even a criminal's death.

All: Mary, we turn to you as our model in suffering and courage. You shared in your Son's suffering and death. Now you share in his resurrection. We, too, share in the cross of Christ, and someday, like you, we will share fully in his resurrection. Help us be patient in our suffering, and to trust in the loving care of our Father in heaven. May those suffering sickness in mind or body experience your Son's healing power. Help us follow his example, and through him, with him, and in him, commend ourselves to the care of our heavenly Father.

Leader: Let us ask Mary to watch over all families.

All: Mother of Perpetual Help, bless our families with your tender, motherly love. May the Sacrament of Marriage bring husbands and wives ever closer together that they may always be faithful, and love each other as Christ loves us. Help all mothers and fathers love and cherish the children God has entrusted to them. May they always be models of a truly Christian life. Help all children, that they may love and respect their parents. Inspire all people to value Christian marriage and family life. Give us a sense of responsibility that we may do our part in making our homes havens of love and peace. Mary, our model, help every family grow daily in genuine love for God and neighbour so that justice and peace may flourish everywhere in the human family.

Leader: From the first moment of her existence, the Holy Spirit filled Mary with his love. By his power, she became the Virgin-Mother of God. Through the same Holy Spirit, she became the perfect wife, the perfect mother. Let us imitate her generosity, her openness to the Holy Spirit, and say,

All: Come, Holy Spirit. Fill our hearts with with your joy and your peace, with your power and your love, with your constant presence within us.

Leader: Receive the Holy Spirit. May he be with you to strengthen you, above you to protect you, before you to lead you, behind you to encourage you, within you to possess you totally. Through the prayers of our holy patron, St Alphonsus, through the intercession of Our Mother of Perpetual Help, through the merits of Our Lord and Saviour Jesus Christ, present in the Most Blessed Sacrament of the altar, may the blessing of almighty God, the Father, Son, and Holy Spirit, descend upon you and remain forever.

All: Amen.

~ The Simple Novena ~

Prayer to Our Lady

O Mary, Mother of Perpetual Succour, I salute you with the most profound veneration and filial devotion. I renew the consecration of myself and all I have to you. I thank you for your maternal protection for the many blessings that I have received through your mercy and most powerful intercession. In all my necessities I have recourse to you, with unbounded confidence. O Help of Christians, O Mother of Mercy, I beseech you now to hear my prayer and to obtain for me from your Divine Son the favour that I request in this novena. (*Here mention your petition.*)

Obtain for me, also, dearest Mother, the grace that I may imitate you and become more like you in the practice of the virtues of humility, purity, submission to the will of God, and charity. Be my protectress in life, guard and guide me in dangers, direct me in perplexities, lead me in the way of perfection, and assist me in the hour of my death, that I may come to Jesus, and with you enjoy him, bless him, and love him eternally in heaven. Amen.

Nine Prayers for a Novena

First day

Blessed be our God who has made you, O Mary, so powerful, so compassionate and ready to succour. What would become of us poor sinners, without you? After having so often deserved disgrace and punishment, how could we go before our sovereign judge, and ask not only pardon, but favours, and a part in eternal glory? Blessed are you, O clement Queen, for having so often stood between me and the punishment I deserve and obtained for me so many precious graces. So whenever I feel the weight of my unworthiness, when all seems lost, and I am tempted to despair, then, full of confidence, I will invoke your blessed name. I will make a claim on your mercy. I will believe that if God lets me feel my weakness, it is to force me to cast myself in the arms of his mercy - on you, my sweet and only hope. Deign to remember this resolution in my time of need, and grant that I may be faithful to it, till my last breath. Mother of Perpetual Succour, grant that I may not cease to have recourse to you. Amen.

Second day

How sweet it is to think, that by your peerless beauty, O Holy Virgin, you have ravished the heart not of any earthly ruler but of the King of Kings, and Creator of the

Universe! You were deemed worthy to be the Mother of the Incarnate Word, the dispenser of his grace, and the cause of our joy. And now, enthroned at the right hand of your Son, you draw to yourself all the hearts of the saints and angels in heaven, and of the just on earth. I rejoice to see you the most beloved of all creatures, since you are the most worthy of love. But, I beg you, O glorious Queen, do not forget me, poor exile that I am, mourning and weeping in this valley of tears. You are raised on high to be the better able to see those who suffer here below and you are made so powerful the more readily to succour us. You know how I am tempted. Be my perpetual succour; watch over me continually, or I shall be lost. May this always be the cry of my heart - Mother of Perpetual Succour, do not forget me. Amen.

Third day

O Mother of my God and Saviour, Jesus Christ, you are indeed my true Mother, and I am indeed your child. What happiness for me to think of you and to be able to call you my Mother. To be called your child is far dearer to me than the honour and dignity of any name on earth. But how utterly unworthy am I of so holy a Mother and how ashamed you could be of a child like me. You are pure as light, pious, humble, full of charity and sweetness; your heart full of divine love; and I am dirty with countless sins, attached to the earth, proud, harsh to my brothers and sisters, and cold towards God. O my Mother, I detest my iniquities - obtain for me pardon; I groan under my miseries, and I spread them before your pitying eyes, that you may cure them. Make me resemble you, save me from my evil inclinations, particularly from (*name it*). O my Mother, my Mother Mary, come to my help. Be my Mother, and make me your worthy child. Amen.

Fourth day

O hope of the wretched, grant that by the merits of Jesus Christ and through your intercession, I shall be saved. Such is my confidence, O Mary, that if my eternal salvation were in my own hands, I would place it in yours; for I trust more in your mercy and protection than in all my own endeavours. My Mother and my hope, do not abandon me as I deserve; be moved to pity; succour me and save me; let all see that your goodness surpasses the number and the malice of my sins. It is testified throughout the Church, that no one under your protection can ever perish. O Mother of Perpetual Succour, say to God that I am your servant and that you defend me, then I shall be saved. O Mary, I put my trust in you. I wish to live and die saying that after God you are my chief hope. Our Lady of Perpetual Succour, grant that I always hope in you. Amen.

Fifth day

O Mary, above all obtain for me the grace to love Jesus Christ, your Divine Son, as he has loved me. You wish him to be loved by all and this is the grace I seek above all others. You can obtain for me the grace to love God. Pray for me, O Mother of Perpetual Succour, and do not stop praying until you see a great love for Jesus enkindled in my soul; or rather do not stop until you see me united with yourself in loving him with a pure and endless love in paradise.

Sixth day

O most tender and compassionate of mothers, turn your eyes of mercy upon me, and lend a gracious ear to my humble prayer. It is true I deserve your rejection because of the ingratitude I have shown to God; but, O Mother of Perpetual Succour, St Bernard assures me that you are always ready to listen to those who pray to you, and you look at our misery and our confidence rather than our merits. Incline then towards me that heart of yours so full of grace. O Mother of God and of men, grant me a share in those rich graces which God has given to you for the whole world's benefit. I have constant need of your succour, which you on your part have a still greater desire to give. I wish that every beat of my heart were an act of love towards you, of confidence in you, and of prayer to you, for myself and for all who are dear to me. O Mother of Perpetual Succour, in you I hope and I shall not be disappointed. Amen.

Seventh day

Most holy Mother of our Saviour, you alone have loved him worthily, for you have not loved him only in word, but in deed and in truth. You have loved us with a love which, next to his own, never had an equal; and which brought you to sacrifice everything, even Jesus himself, for us. O Mother of Perpetual Succour, obtain for me a heart like that of Jesus and your own, so that I may be meek and humble, patient, compassionate, more ready to forgive than to take offence, and to give than to receive; that I may keep my eyes open to my own faults, and may close them to those of my neighbour; that I may put up with everything rather than cause pain to another; that severe to myself, I may be full of indulgence towards others; that I may love them in Jesus, and Jesus in them; that by my prayers, my good advice and good example, I may strive to draw them for their salvation to Jesus and to you. Amen.

Eighth day

O Mary, Lily of the Valley and Mirror of Purity, blessed by God, whose infinite goodness has given us in you so powerful a means of deliverance from the slavery of lust. How many you have preserved in chastity. How many, after having long been slaves of their shameful passions, have, through you, recovered their freedom. I beg you, then, preserve me and all who belong to me from the attacks of this vice. You defend all those who confide in your perpetual succour, and who invoke you in the hour of danger; grant, then, that I remember to call on you when the enemy of my salvation assails me. This is the grace I ask of you; by your holy Virginity and your Immaculate Conception obtain for me, O Mother of Perpetual Succour, purity of body and soul. Amen.

Ninth day

O Mother of Perpetual Succour, in you alone is my hope, for you are the advocate of sinners and patron of the dying. I place myself from now on in your blessed hands, I entrust to you the care of my sinful soul. May a peaceful and holy death be the crowning answer to all the prayers I address to you from now to the end of my days. When my last hour comes grant that I may receive all the succours the Holy Church affords to the dying; and be pleased yourself to come then to my aid, to encourage, console and defend me. Grant that your blessed name, with that of Jesus, may be my last thought and my last sigh. Come, O Lady of Perpetual Succour, to succour me at the hour of my death. Amen.

―More Prayers to―
Our Lady of Perpetual Succour

Prayers for Mary's Protection

Mother of Perpetual Succour, blessed and favoured by the Father, you became not only the Mother of the Redeemer, but Mother of the redeemed as well. We come to you today as your loving children. Watch over us and take care of us. As you held the child Jesus in your loving arms, so take us in your arms. Be a mother ready at every moment to help us. Intercede for us, dear Mother, in obtaining pardon for our sins, love for Jesus, final perseverance, and the grace always to call upon you. Amen.

O Holy Virgin Mary, Mother of Perpetual Succour, I implore you to come to my aid always and everywhere; in my temptations; after my falls; in my difficulties and, above all, at the hour of my death. Give me, loving Mother, the desire, the habit, always to have recourse to you, for I feel assured that if I invoke you you will come to my assistance. Obtain for me, then, this grace of graces, the grace to pray to you without ceasing, and with child-like confidence, that by virtue of this faithful prayer I may ensure your Perpetual Succour.

Bless me, O loving Mother, and pray for me now and at the hour of my death. Amen.

O Holy Virgin Mary, Mother of Perpetual Succour, always shield the Church with your protection. Through the infinite merits of Jesus Christ, which we offer by you to the Eternal Father, obtain for sinners the grace of a holy death, for the souls of our deceased relations the grace of deliverance from the flames of purgatory, and for all of us the grace of pardon and of abundant mercy. Amen.

Prayer for Grace

O Mother of Perpetual Succour, with the greatest confidence I come before your sacred picture, in order to invoke your aid. You have seen the wounds which Jesus has been pleased to receive for our sake; you have seen the blood of your Son flowing for our salvation; you know how much your Son desires to apply to us the fruit of his redemption. Behold, I cast myself at your feet, and pray you to obtain for my soul the grace I stand so much in need of. O Mary, most loving of all mothers, obtain for me from the Heart of Jesus, the source of every good, this grace (*mention it*). O Mother of Perpetual Succour, you desire our salvation far more than we do ourselves; your Son has given you to us for our Mother; you have yourself chosen to be called Mother of Perpetual Succour. Show me then that you love me, show that you are really my Mother, show that you are justly called Mother of Perpetual Succour. I do not trust in my merits, but in your powerful intercession; I trust in your goodness, I trust in your motherly love. Mother of Perpetual Succour, for the love you bear to Jesus your Son and my Redeemer, for the love of your great servant Alphonsus, for the love of my soul obtain for me the grace I ask from you. Amen.

Prayer in Suffering

O Mother of Perpetual Succour, numerous clients continually surround your holy picture, all imploring your mercy. All bless you as the assured succour of the miserable; all feel the benefit of your maternal protection. With confidence, then, I present myself before you in my misery. See, dear Mother, the many evils to which we are exposed; see how numerous are our wants. Trials and sorrows often depress us; reverses of fortune and privations, often grievous, bring misery into our homes; everywhere we meet the cross. Have pity, compassionate Mother, on us and on our families; and especially in this my necessity (*mention it*) from which I now suffer. Help me, O my Mother, in my distress; deliver me from my ills; or if it be the will of God that I should endure them, let me suffer with love and patience. This grace I expect of you with confidence, because you are our Perpetual Succour. Amen.

Prayer in Sickness

O dear Mother of Perpetual Succour, see how much I suffer from this sickness. Together with the body, my soul is also afflicted. I have not even strength to pray as I ought to do. Nothing is able to give me any relief. Even the visits and compassion of my best friends do not give me any comfort. My courage begins to fail; impatience and sadness oppress my soul. In my great distress I put all my trust in you, most tender of all mothers. Your compassionate heart will certainly have pity on me; yes, most merciful Mother, you will not forget your poor afflicted child. Obtain, then, for me courage and strength to accept all these trials from the hand of God with patience and faith. If it is for the good of my soul, grant that I may recover my former health; but if it is the will of God that I should suffer still longer, or that this sickness should lead me to a better life, I am perfectly at peace, for I am sure that you, O loving Mother, will obtain for me the grace to do whatever God asks of me.

Prayer for Financial Help

Mary, our Mother, we know that you are our Perpetual Help, not only in our spiritual need but in our material need as well. With humble heart and childlike confidence we beg you to help us in our dire need, since we cannot meet our just debts. Dear Mother, we are not asking for wealth or prosperity, but merely for help in satisfying our pressing obligations. You are the Queen of heaven and earth and as such, the dispenser of so many favours granted by your Son, Jesus. We know you are most kind and generous to all your devoted children. Loving Mother, we plead with you to obtain the financial help we so desperately need in our present situation. We thank you, dear Mother, and promise to make your Perpetual Help known far and wide. Amen.

Prayer for the conversion of a sinner

O Mary, Mother of Perpetual Succour, you know so well the great value of an immortal soul. You know what it means, that every soul has been redeemed by the blood of your Divine Son, you will not then despise my prayer, if I ask from you the conversion of a sinner. You, O Merciful Mother, know his/her irregular life. I know that you are the refuge of sinners and that God has given you power to bring about the conversion of even the most wretched sinners. You have converted so many sinners at the intercession of their friends and family. Please listen to my prayer, and bring (*name*) conversion of heart. O Mary, help; O Mother of Perpetual Succour, show that you are the advocate and refuge of sinners. Amen.

Prayer to the most Blessed Virgin Mary

O Blessed Virgin Mary! Who can duly thank you, or herald forth your praises, you who by the assent of your single will, rescued a fallen world? What honour can be paid to you by our weak human nature, which, by your intervention alone, has found the way to return to grace and life? Accept, then, such poor thanks as we have here to offer, unequal to your merits though they be; and, accepting our good desires, obtain by your prayers the remission of our offences. Graciously hear our prayers, and obtain for us the remedy of reconciliation. May the offering we make to God, through you, be acceptable in his sight; and may that be granted which we ask with trustful hearts. Accept our offerings, grant our petitions, banish our fears, for you are the sole hope of sinners. Through you we hope for the forgiveness of our sins, and in you, most Blessed Lady, is the hope of our reward. Holy Mary, succour the miserable, help the faint-hearted, console those that weep, pray for the people, be the advocate of the clergy, intercede for religious women; be at hand, ready to aid our prayers, and obtain for us what we need. Make it your care, Blessed Lady, always to intercede for the people of God - you who were worthy to bear the Redeemer of the world, who lives and reigns for ever and ever. Amen.

Memorare

Remember, O most gracious Virgin Mary, that never was it known that anyone who fled to thy protection, implored thy help or sought thy intercession was left unaided. Inspired by this confidence I fly unto thee, O Virgin of virgins, my Mother. To thee do I come, before thee I stand, sinful and sorrowful. O Mother of the Word Incarnate, despise not my petitions but in thy mercy hear and answer me.

Mother of Perpetual Succour, pray for us
Mater de Perpetuo Succursu, ora pro nobis.
Amen.

Prayer to St Michael

Holy Michael Archangel, defend us in the day of battle. Be our safeguard against the wickedness and snares of the devil. May God rebuke him, we humbly pray, and do thou, Prince of the heavenly host, by the power of God, thrust down to hell Satan and all wicked spirits who wander through the world for the ruin of souls. Amen.

Prayer to St Gabriel

O Blessed Archangel Gabriel, we beseech thee, do thou intercede for us at the throne of divine mercy in our present necessities, that as thou didst announce to Mary the mystery of the Incarnation, so through thy prayers and patronage in heaven we may obtain the benefits of the same, and sing the praise of God forever in the land of the living. Amen.

Prayer to St Alphonsus to obtain a great devotion to Our Lady of Perpetual Succour

O St Alphonsus, most faithful servant of Mary, you who know how much this good Mother deserves to be loved, honoured and served, make me, I pray you, understand her sublime privileges in order to admire, praise and love her, and her eminent virtues in order to imitate them.

O my holy protector, I wish to serve Mary as you have served her, to love her as much as you have loved her, to praise her as you have praised her, and to become as dear to her heart as yourself. But the accomplishment of this desire is, I confess, far above my own power; my heart is too much attached to earthly things to rise so high; so I address myself to you, my powerful advocate, and I beg of you to obtain for me at least the grace to love Mary, to honour and serve her with all my strength; and above all the grace always to invoke her under the consoling title of Mother of Perpetual Succour. Amen.

Glory be to the Father (three times)

V. Pray for us St Alphonsus Mary.

R. That we may be made worthy of the promises of Christ.

Prayer of St Alphonsus Liguori

Mother, most holy and immaculate Virgin, mother of my Lord, Queen of the universe, advocate, hope, and refuge of sinners, I come to you today. I who am unworthy render you my most humble homage, O Great Queen, and I thank you for all the graces you have obtained for me, and in particular for having saved me from hell which I have so often deserved. I love you; and, for the love which I bear you, I promise to serve you always and do all in my power to make others love you. I place in you all my hope and I confide my salvation to your care. Accept me as your servant and receive me under your mantle, O Mother of Mercy. And since you are so powerful with God, deliver me from all temptations, or, rather, obtain for me the strength to triumph over them until death. I ask of you a perfect love for Jesus Christ; through you I hope to die a good death. O my Mother, by the love which you bear God, I beseech you to help me at all times but especially at the last moment of my life. Do not leave me, I beg you until you see me safe in heaven, blessing you and singing your mercies for all eternity. Amen.

~ DAILY DEVOTIONS ~

Morning prayers

Omy God, I believe that you are here present; I adore your supreme majesty; I love your infinite goodness above all things; I thank you for all the graces you have bestowed on me until now, and especially for having preserved me during this night. I offer to you all my thoughts, words, actions and sufferings of this day; I unite them to those of Jesus Christ; and I desire to act with the sole motive of pleasing you, and in honour of:

Sunday - all my Holy Patrons;
Monday - my Guardian Angel;
Tuesday - the Infant Jesus;
Wednesday - St Joseph;
Thursday - the Most Holy Sacrament;
Friday - the Sacred Passion of Jesus Christ;
Saturday - the Most Blessed Virgin Mary.

I form the intention of praying for the souls in purgatory. I offer all my good works for the purpose of obtaining the virtue of (*here mention some particular virtue which you most desire to acquire; for example, charity, patience, humility etc.*). O my God, for the love of Jesus Christ, preserve me from all sin. O my Jesus, by your merits, grant me the grace to live united to you. O Mary, my Mother, bless me, and keep me under your mantle. My Guardian Angel, my holy patrons, pray for me. Amen.

Our Father, Hail Mary, I believe in God.

Then three Hail Marys in honour of the Immaculate Conception of Mary, to obtain purity of soul and body, and add:

O Mary, Mother of Perpetual Succour, pray for me. My protector, St Alphonsus, in all my wants make me have recourse to Mary.

Night prayers

In the name of the Father, and of the Son, and of the Holy Spirit. Amen.

Blessed be the holy and undivided Trinity, now and for ever. Amen.

Our Father, Hail Mary, I believe in God.

Come O Holy Spirit, fill the hearts of your faithful, and kindle in them the fire of your love.

V.   Send forth your Spirit and they shall be created.
R.   And you shall renew the face of the earth.

Let us pray. O God, who has taught the hearts of the faithful by the light of the Holy Spirit, grant that, by the gift of the same Spirit, we may be always truly wise, and ever rejoice in his consolation. Through Christ our Lord. Amen.

Let us place ourselves in the presence of God, and give him thanks for all the benefits which we have received from him, particularly today.

O my God, I firmly believe that you are here, and perfectly see me, and that you observe all my actions, all my thoughts, and the most secret motions of my heart. You watch over me with an incomparable love, every moment bestowing favours and preserving me from evil. Blessed be your holy name, and may all creatures bless your goodness for the benefits which I have ever received from you, and particularly today. May the saints and angels make up for my defects in giving you due thanks. Never permit me to repay your bounties with ingratitude, and your blessings with offences and injuries.

Let us ask our Lord Jesus Christ the grace to discover the sins which we have committed today, and beg of him a true sorrow for them, and a sincere repentance.

O my Lord Jesus Christ, judge of the living and dead, before whom I must appear one day to give an exact account of my whole life; enlighten me, I beg you, and give me a humble and contrite heart, that I may see where I have offended your infinite majesty; and judge myself now with such a just severity, that then you may judge me with mercy and clemency.

Let us here examine what sins we have committed today, by thought, word, deed or omission. (If you cannot think of any sin you have committed today, renew your sorrow for the sins of your past life). Let us conceive a great sorrow for having offended God.

O my God, I detest these and all other sins which I have committed against your divine majesty. I am extremely sorry that I have offended you, because you are infinitely good, and sin displeases you. I love you with my whole heart, and firmly propose, by the help of your grace, never more to offend you. I resolve to avoid the occasions of sin; I will confess my sins, and will endeavour to make reparation for them. Have mercy on me, O God, have mercy, and pardon me, a wretched sinner. In the name of your beloved Son, Jesus, I humbly beg you to wash me with his Precious Blood so that my sins may be entirely remitted.

Say the Hail Holy Queen to our Blessed Lady for the grace of a happy death, then three Hail Marys as in the morning.

Jesus, Mary and Joseph, I give you my heart and my soul.

Jesus, Mary and Joseph, assist me in my last agony.

Jesus, Mary and Joseph, may I breathe forth my soul
  in peace with you.

O Mary, conceived without sin, pray for us who
  have recourse to you.

Holy Mary, deliver us from the pains of hell.

Holy Mary, Our Lady of Deliverance, pray for us and
  for the holy souls in purgatory.

Mother of Perpetual Succour, pray for us.

The Mysteries of the Holy Rosary
An intention for each Mystery

The Joyful Mysteries

The Annunciation - Humility

The Visitation - Fraternal Charity

The Nativity - Love of God

The Presentation - Obedience

The Finding of Jesus in the Temple - the Holy Father

The Mysteries of Light

The Baptism of the Lord - Children
The Wedding at Cana - Married Couples
The Proclamation of the Kingdom of God and the Call
  to Conversion - Evangelization
The Transfiguration - Conversion of Heart
The Institution of the Eucharist - Priests and Vocations

The Sorrowful Mysteries

The Agony in the Garden - Fervour in Prayer
The Scourging of Jesus - Patience
The Crowning with Thorns - Conversion of Sinners
Jesus Carries His Cross - Holy Souls
The Crucifixion and Death of Jesus - the Dying

The Glorious Mysteries

The Resurrection - a Happy Death
The Ascension of Jesus into Heaven
  - Exaltation of the Church
The Descent of the Holy Spirit - Gifts of the Holy Spirit
The Assumption of our Lady into Heaven
  - Devotion to Mary
The Coronation of the Blessed Virgin Mary
  - Perseverance

Prayer

O God, whose only-begotten Son, by his life, death and resurrection, has purchased for us the rewards of eternal life; grant, we beseech you, that, meditating upon these mysteries of the most Holy Rosary of the Blessed Virgin Mary, we may both imitate what they contain, and obtain what they promise. Through the same Christ our Lord. Amen.

~ Hymn ~

O Mother Blessed

Composed by St Alphonsus Liguori,
translated by E. Vaughan.

O Mother blest, whom God bestows
On sinners and on just
What joy, what hope thou givest those
Who in thy mercy trust.

Thou art clement, thou art chaste
Mary, thou art fair;
Of all mothers, sweetest, best,
None with thee compare.

O heavenly Mother, mistress sweet!
It never yet was told
That suppliant sinner left thy feet
Unpitied, unconsoled.

O Mother, pitiful and mild
Cease not to pray for me:
For I so love thee as a child,
And sigh for love of thee.

Most powerful Mother, all men know
Thy Son denies thee naught:
Thou askest, wishest it, and lo!
His power thy will hath wrought.

O Mother blest, for me obtain,
Ungrateful though I be,
To love that God who first could deign
To show such love for me.